A RUSSIAN JEWISH FAMILY

JOURNEY BETWEEN • TWO WORLDS •

A RUSSIAN JEWISH FAMILY

By Jane Mersky Leder

Lerner Publications Company • Minneapolis

The interviews for this book were conducted in the fall of 1994 and in 1995.

This book is available in two editions:
Library binding by Lerner Publications Company
Soft cover by First Avenue Editions
241 First Avenue North
Minneapolis, MN 55401
ISBN: 0–8225–3401–0 (lib. bdg.)
ISBN: 0–8225–9744–6 (pbk.)

LIBRARY OF CONGRESS CATALOGING-IN-PUBLICATION DATA

Leder, Jane Mersky.
    A Russian Jewish family / by Jane Mersky Leder.
      p. cm. — (Journey between two worlds)
    Summary: Describes one Jewish family's fourteen year struggle to emigrate from Leningrad in the Soviet Union to Chicago, Illinois, and the adjustments they have made.
    ISBN 0–8225–3401–0 (lib. bdg. : alk. paper)
    1. Jews, Soviet—Illinois—Chicago—Juvenile literature. 2. Jews—Soviet Union—Juvenile literature. 3. Refusenicks—Juvenile literature. 4. Immigrants—Illinois—Chicago—Juvenile literature. [1. Jews—Soviet Union. 2. Jews—United States. 3. Immigrants—United States. 4. United States—Emigration and immigration.]
    I. Title. II. Series.
    F548.9.J5L43 1996
    977.3'11004924047—dc20   95–38544

Manufactured in the United States of America
1 2 3 4 5 6 – JR – 01 00 99 98 97 96

AUTHOR'S NOTE

What makes my job as a writer so special is the chance to meet wonderful and interesting people. And the Shurov family—Boris, Nick, Michael, and Irene—as well as Tatyana and Lev Kozinoze, are *very* special. Imagine the many challenges of immigrating to a new country. Then imagine letting a stranger into your life. That stranger wants to know everything about you. She keeps asking questions about life in the old country and life in the United States. There are phone calls, visits, photo shoots, and more photo shoots. Hours and hours of precious time are spent sharing your life and all its secrets.

To the entire Shurov family—Alan [the photographer] and I are so grateful for the opportunity to have shared a slice of your lives. You made us laugh and marvel and even cry. But, most of all, you enriched our lives with your friendship, a friendship that will last long after this book is published.

And to the memory of Lev, a man who could not speak a word of English but whose energy and spirit spoke for themselves. It is our loss that our time together was so short.

This book is dedicated to Lev Kozinoze, who passed away in the fall of 1995.

Vendors sell literature on a busy street in Saint Petersburg, Russia. For more than 70 years, the Soviet government determined what materials could be printed in Russia and other republics of the former Soviet Union.

SERIES INTRODUCTION

 What they have left behind is sometimes a living nightmare of war and hunger that most Americans can hardly begin to imagine. As refugees set out to start a new life in another country, they are torn by many feelings. They may wish they didn't have to leave their homeland. They may fear giving up the only life they have ever known. Many may also feel excitement and hope as they struggle to build a better life in a new country.

People who move from one place to another are called migrants. Two types of migrants are immigrants and refugees. Immigrants choose to leave their homelands, usually to improve their standards of living. They may be leaving behind poverty, famine (hunger), or a failing economy. They may be pursuing a better job or reuniting with family members.

Refugees, on the other hand, often have no choice but to flee their homeland to protect their own personal safety. How could anyone be in so much danger?

The Soviet Union frequently staged military parades to demonstrate the importance it placed on the nation's armed forces.

(Left) *Once the headquarters of the Soviet regime, the Kremlin of Moscow houses the Russian government.* (Below) *The Soviets built many monuments to Vladimir Lenin, the founder of the Soviet Union.*

The government of his or her country is either unable or unwilling to protect its citizens from persecution, or cruel treatment. In many cases, the government is actually the cause of the persecution. Government leaders or another group within the country may be persecuting anyone of a certain race, religion, or ethnic background. Or they may persecute those who belong to a particular social group or who hold political opinions that are not accepted by the government.

From the 1950s through the mid-1970s, the number of refugees worldwide held steady at between 1.5 and 2.5 million. The number began to rise sharply in 1976. By the mid-1990s, it approached 20 million. These figures do not include people who are fleeing disasters such as famine (estimated to be at least 10 million). Nor do they include those who are forced to leave their homes but stay within their own countries (about 27 million).

As this rise in refugees and other migrants continues, countries that have long welcomed newcomers are beginning to close their doors. Some U.S. citizens question whether the United States should accept refugees when it cannot even meet the needs of all its own people. On the other hand, experts point out that the number of refugees is small—less than 20 percent of all migrants worldwide—so refugees really don't have a very big impact on the nation. Still others suggest that the tide of refugees could be slowed through greater efforts to address the problems that force people to flee. There are no easy answers in this ongoing debate.

This book is one in a series called *Journey Between Two Worlds*, which looks at the lives of refugee families—their difficulties and triumphs. Each book describes the journey of a family from their homeland to the United States and how they adjust to a new life in America while still preserving traditions from their homeland. The series makes no attempt to join the debate about refugees. Instead, *Journey Between Two Worlds* hopes to give readers a better understanding of the daily struggles and joys of a refugee family.

Children in Moscow play on a homemade go-cart.

The Shurov family, including Boris (far left), Irene, and Michael came to the United States from Russia in 1990.

Boris Shurov, age twelve, loves basketball. Michael Jordan is his favorite player. When Jordan quit basketball in 1993, he broke Boris's heart. "I don't want to talk about it," Boris said then. Eighteen months later, Jordan changed his mind and started playing basketball again with the Chicago Bulls. "I was so surprised," Boris says. "I didn't think he would ever play again. I took him at his word. Am I glad? You bet I am!"

Boris was born in Russia, a European country that for more than 70 years was part of the former Soviet Union. As a little boy, Boris knew nothing about basketball. He had never played the game nor seen anyone else play it.

Beginning in 1990, however, basketball courts became a familiar place for Boris. In that year, Boris, then seven, and his family immigrated to the United States.

An industrial and cultural center, Saint Petersburg was founded in the early 1700s by Czar Peter I as the capital of the Russian Empire.

He didn't understand why he had to move. He liked his home in Leningrad (now called Saint Petersburg). School was fun, and he had many friends. Compared to most Russians, his parents made a lot of money. "It was a sad day when I said good-bye," Boris recalls.

Boris was too young to know about the problems that led his parents, Michael and Irene, to want to move to another country. In 1976, before Boris was born, Michael had tried unsuccessfully to leave Russia. Thus he became what is known as a refusenik. This meant the Soviet government had refused him permission to emigrate.

Michael wanted to emigrate because he yearned for more personal freedom. He was a film director, but the Soviet government would not let him produce the kinds of movies he wanted to make. "I could not express myself freely," Michael says. "I wanted to leave."

"The years before we left were terrible," Michael remembers. "I was fired from three different jobs just because I was a refusenik. Each time I was fired, I made less money. And I worried that the KGB [secret police] would come to my home.

"We had a neighbor who lived in the same building. He, too, was a refusenik. He was put in prison. Then he came home. But the KGB came to his house two times a week. They asked what he was doing. They wanted to know what he was thinking. He had no freedom. I wanted freedom. That is why I dreamed of coming to America."

Irene and Michael tell the author (left) about the events that led them to become political refugees in the United States.

Michael and Irene didn't talk about problems in front of Boris and his older brother, Nick. Nick had no idea his father was a refusenik. In fact, Nick didn't even know what a refusenik was. He thought his parents were happy. Nick assumed he and his family would live in Russia forever.

Boris had never dreamed of going to the United States. "I didn't even know where America was," Boris says. Nick knew a little about the United States. He had heard it was a nice place where it was easy to buy nice things. "But life was good for me in Russia," Nick recalls. "My parents had a house and a condominium. We had two cars. We had everything!"

 The Shurovs are Jewish. As Jews, they were not allowed to practice their religion openly in Russia, which has a long history of anti-Semitic (anti-Jewish) laws. In the 1790s, Russian leaders started requiring Jews to settle in select areas of the Russian Empire. These locations were known collectively as the Pale of Settlement.

Beginning in the 1880s, Russian troops repeatedly stormed the Pale. During these attacks, called pogroms, thousands of Jews were killed. The laws requiring Jews to live in the Pale were dropped in the early 1900s. Although many Jews stayed in the Pale, thousands moved to Russia proper, where anti-Semitism still ran high. During World War II (1939–1945), Nazi Germany occupied cities of the former Pale of Settlement. Most of the Jews either fled or were executed.

Although Jews and other groups now have more religious freedom in Russia, Jews still worry about their safety. They can never be sure if or when the government or the people might turn against them again.

Michael and Irene did not educate Nick and Boris about Jewish traditions. The parents were afraid to. "I worried about my children," explains Irene. "I did not want them to have trouble with non-Jewish children. I did not want them to be called bad names like 'dirty Jew.' I was called those names when I was young. It hurt so much."

(Facing page) *While growing up in Russia, Boris* (left) *and Nick were unaware of the political troubles facing their parents.* (Right) *Since coming to Chicago, the boys have learned the whole story.*

Spanning more than 6.5 million square miles (16.8 million square kilometers), Russia is the largest country in the world. Many of Russia's neighboring countries—with the exception of Norway, Finland, Poland, China, Mongolia, and Japan—are former Soviet republics.

A thousand years ago, Russia was a small region in eastern Europe. Russia gradually gained control of many different territories and grew into an empire.

In the 1500s, rulers called czars began to govern Russia. A czar was like an emperor. He alone made all the important decisions concerning the Russian Empire. Most of the czars isolated Russia from the rest of

The Hermitage Museum in Saint Petersburg contains a world-famous collection of artworks.

Europe, where reforms were leading to better lives for many people.

Most Russians were poor, uneducated peasants who were forced to farm the land of the wealthy. The peasants worked hard, relying on the same kinds of hand tools their ancestors had used.

Because Russians were isolated, industrial progress in the country was slow. During the 1800s—a time of great inventions—Russians did not benefit from the new ideas that were improving life for people outside the country. It was as if Russia was standing still in time.

Russia, however, produced many great artists. Writers such as Fyodor Dostoyevsky and composers such as Pyotr Ilich Tchaikovsky entertained thousands. Their books and music are still popular today.

In 1917 a revolution broke out in Russia. The people forced Czar Nicholas II to end his reign. A group called the Communists, who soon murdered the ex-czar and his family, gained power.

Under the leadership of Vladimir Lenin, the new Communist government took control of banks, libraries, and large homes throughout Russia. The Communists outlawed private property. People weren't allowed to own homes, businesses, or farms. The Communists wanted to give the working class as many advantages as the minority of wealthy people in Russia. But with this equality came many losses.

(Facing page, top) *Soldiers oversee Czar Nicholas II during his arrest.* (Facing page, bottom) *A Russian peasant of the early 1900s wore layers of threadbare clothing to keep warm.* (Right) *Hundreds of different ethnic groups lived within the borders of the USSR.*

 Wealthy people, along with other Russians, opposed Lenin. They wanted their homes and businesses back. From 1918 to 1920, a civil war between Communists and anti-Communists tore Russia apart. After two years of fighting, Lenin and the Communist Party reestablished their control. They set up the Union of Soviet Socialist Republics (USSR), or the Soviet Union for short.

The Soviet Union was eventually made up of 15 republics, including Russia. Each republic had its own Communist government. The central government, located in Moscow, Russia, controlled the republics. The Communist Party was the only political party allowed, and its members made all the decisions for the country. Ordinary citizens had very little power and few personal freedoms. Those who openly disagreed with the Communist Party were jailed. Many were even killed.

Joseph Stalin headed the Soviet Union from 1924 to 1953. Although he helped to save his country from defeat during World War II, Stalin was a cruel and untrusting leader. He gave orders to imprison or kill anti-Communists and other people he considered to be

Under the influence of Joseph Stalin (above), *thousands of Russian Jews were evacuated from their hometowns* (right).

his enemies. Millions of innocent people died needlessly under Stalin's rule. Many of them were Jewish. Rulers who came after Stalin were not as harsh, but Communist policies continued to silence those who openly disagreed with the government.

The Soviet government started programs in the 1960s and 1970s to improve industries. The nation's standard of living, however, stayed far behind that of developed countries. The Soviet people continued to face shortages of goods, including food. They stood in long lines every day for bread and other basic items.

By the 1980s, the Soviet Union had become a leading military power. But the country's people still lacked choices and freedoms. Many of the republics were clamoring for independence. They wanted an end to Communist leadership.

A new leader named Mikhail Gorbachev tried to save Communism when he took control of the Soviet Union in 1985. Gorbachev introduced some freedoms to Soviet life. The power of the central government in Moscow was reduced somewhat. Open elections were held for the first time for some political offices. But Gorbachev refused to give the republics their independence.

In 1990 the Soviet republics of Estonia, Latvia, and Lithuania insisted on their freedom. Gorbachev looked the other way while Soviet forces put down the independence movement.

To provide energy to factories and homes, the Soviet government built a pipeline that carries natural gas from Siberia—a huge region covering central and eastern Russia—to the cities of western Russia.

In August 1991, Communist Party leaders who disagreed with Gorbachev's reforms tried unsuccessfully to overthrow the government. Their failure led to the end of the Communist Party in the Soviet Union. By the end of the year, the Soviet Union itself fell apart. Each of the 15 republics gained its independence, and the Soviet Union as a nation ceased to exist.

Russia is the largest of the 15 republics that once made up the Soviet Union. In 1991 Russians voted for their leader for the first time in the country's history. They elected Boris Yeltsin as president. Newspapers, radio, and television are no longer controlled by the state. People can operate their own businesses.

The future of Russia and the other republics is uncertain. Street crime and government corruption are serious problems. Prices for food and clothes have jumped more than 1,000 percent since the breakup of the Soviet Union. Turning government-run businesses over to private citizens is a long, difficult process. People are hopeful that the former Communist country will grow and prosper. Only time will tell.

(Right) *A crowd rallies outside the Kremlin for independence.* (Facing page) *Saint Basil's Church, a Russian landmark, sits next to the Kremlin.*

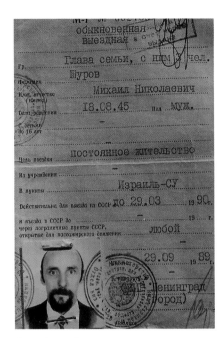

Immigration papers were among the many documents the Shurovs needed to leave the Soviet Union.

 Time and patience paid off for the Shurovs. The Soviet government under Gorbachev was allowing many refuseniks to emigrate. In 1990, after 14 years, Michael's dream came true. The family finally received word that they could go. But they had to leave so much behind.

"The government made it as hard as possible for us to leave," Irene remarks. "We could only take a limited amount of our belongings with us . . . . We put all the clothes that could fit into six or seven suitcases. We were forced to sell everything else except a piano and some paintings that we shipped to America. We [had] money, but the government only let us take $200 out of Russia."

Hardest of all, the Shurovs left behind good friends and relatives. Michael's brother and sister remained. So did Irene's parents. They were not ready to leave their homeland. At least, not yet.

The journey from Russia to America was not direct. The Shurovs had to do a lot of paperwork, and the first travel papers only allowed them to go to Austria. They spent a month there before going to Italy for another two months.

"It was not our idea to take such a journey," Irene says. "But we had no other choice. An [international] Jewish organization knew we had very little money and helped us. It paid for our food and one room for the whole family."

The Colosseum is one of many famous ruins in Rome, Italy, a city the Shurovs lived in briefly before moving to the United States.

"We were free!" Michael exclaims. "That was the important thing. We were not in America, but we were free."

"It was not too bad," Boris recalls. "We lived in a hotel and then in a small apartment. There were other Russian immigrants there. It was like family."

That "family" helped when Nick had an accident on his bike. "My son had a lot of energy," Irene remembers. "He was riding his bike too fast. He ran into a car." Nick hit the car hard. He broke one of the windows and got a concussion, or injury to the brain. Luckily, he had to go to the hospital for tests only. The doctors let him go home to recover.

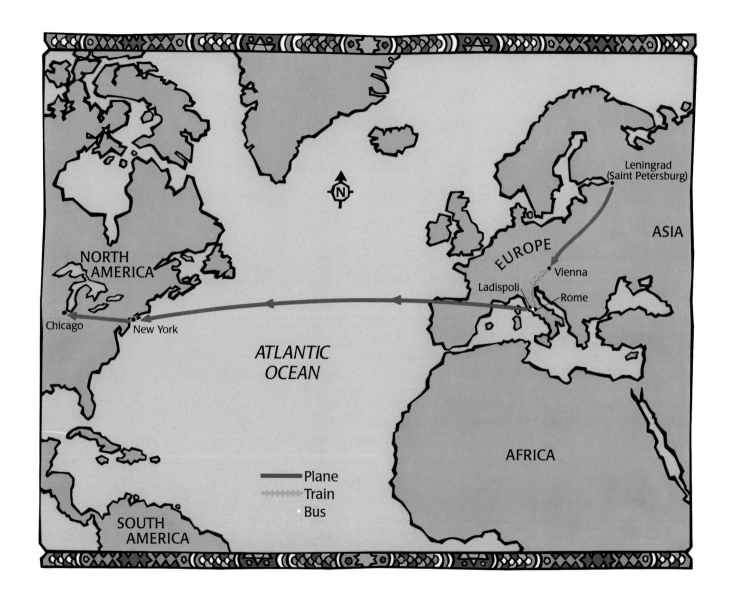

 Finally, after three months in Europe, the Shurovs flew to their new home in Chicago, Illinois. "My father has a cousin here in Chicago," Boris says. "She gave us the invitation to come." (Laws in the United States require that refugees have an invitation.)

The first thing Boris remembers about his new home is Chicago–O'Hare International Airport. "It is so big and nice," he says.

Irene recalls how surprised she was to visit downtown Chicago. "All we heard about in Russia was the

(Facing page) *The Shurovs journeyed from Saint Petersburg to Austria and then Italy before coming to the United States.* (Above left) *Boris's first memory of the United States is the terminal of Chicago–O'Hare International Airport.* (Above) *Skyscrapers line the streets of downtown Chicago.*

Like many other students in the United States, Boris does his homework on a computer.

gangster Al Capone. He was the head of [a criminal organization called] the Mafia. But that was many years ago. Nobody [in Russia] knows what Chicago is like today."

Irene thinks Chicago resembles Saint Petersburg in some ways. "Both cities have a lot of culture and art," she notes. "And the buildings are beautiful. Chicago is a very nice place to live. I am happy to be here."

 None of the Shurovs knew how to speak English when they arrived in Chicago. Well, that is not exactly true. "I knew ten words," Boris jokes. "I knew words like *lion* and *cow*. But those words didn't help me. I was frustrated. I could not speak English. And I did not know anyone."

Boris was lucky. His family rented an apartment in an area of Chicago called Rogers Park. Many other Russian immigrants lived close by. They all went to the same school, where one of the teachers spoke both Russian and English. She taught a special class for Boris and other Russian-speakers. "I took classes in Russian," Boris says. "At the same time, I learned English."

Boris has adjusted like any other American kid. He takes all of his classes in English. "I still speak Russian at home," Boris explains. "I read Russian, too."

(Left) *Shortly after arriving in Chicago, the Shurovs moved into this brownstone apartment building.* (Bottom) *Boris has made many friends since moving to the United States, including a few Russians with backgrounds similar to his.*

Boris and his mother still read Russian together several times each week. They often pick up a Swedish folktale by Astrid Lindgren that has been translated into Russian. Called *Carlson Who Lives on the Roof*, the book has remained Boris's favorite folktale since he was a little boy.

"It's about a boy who makes friends with a man who can fly," Boris explains. "The man's name is Carlson. Of course, the boy's parents don't think the man is real. They think their son has imagined him. But they change their minds when they see him with their own eyes. The boy's babysitter is afraid of ghosts. Carlson and the boy dress in white sheets and scare her. It is very funny. The funny thing is I don't remember how the story ends. I'll tell you when we finish reading it."

Now that Boris is 12, he doesn't read many folktales. He likes adventure stories such as the Hardy Boys series. And he likes scary books, too.

(Facing page) *Boris and his mother read a book together in Russian.* (Above) *Later he completes a jigsaw puzzle.*

A teenager when his family moved to the United States, Nick is studying hard to earn the equivalent of a high-school diploma.

 Boris's brother, Nick, is 20. Nick dropped out of high school during his junior year. "Language was not the problem," Nick says. "My English is very good. I just wasn't interested in the classes I had to take. I was much more interested in automobile mechanics. But my high school didn't have those classes. If we had stayed in Russia, I would have graduated. I was an okay student. I didn't have any big problems."

After dropping out of school, Nick worked at a small grocery store for many months. He has since left that job to study for the GED, or General Educational Development tests, to earn the equivalent of a high-school diploma. "I want to join the army," Nick declares. "And they require a high-school diploma or a GED. I have a tutor and will take the [GED]."

Would Nick ever fight in a war against the Russians? "That's a tough one," Nick sighs. "No . . . no, I could not fight against them. Russia is where I was born. I still have friends and relatives there."

However, if given the choice, Nick would not move back to Russia. "I would *love* to visit," he says. "But there is more freedom here in America. I have more choices. I would lose everything if I were to move back."

One of Nick's favorite pastimes is working on his car.

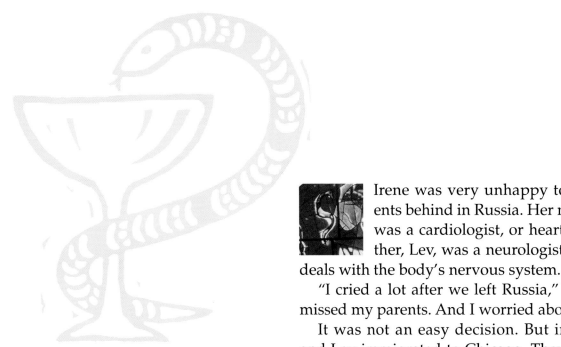

 Irene was very unhappy to leave her parents behind in Russia. Her mother, Tatyana, was a cardiologist, or heart doctor. Her father, Lev, was a neurologist—a doctor who deals with the body's nervous system.

"I cried a lot after we left Russia," Irene recalls. "I missed my parents. And I worried about them."

It was not an easy decision. But in 1993, Tatyana and Lev immigrated to Chicago. They could not bear living so far away from their daughter and her family. Irene is their only child. Boris and Nick are their only grandchildren.

Unlike the Shurovs, neither Tatyana nor Lev speaks English. And learning another language gets more difficult with age. As a result, their lives in America are not as full as they were in Russia. Because they do not know English, they cannot practice medicine here. They have a lot of free time. Tatyana spends most of her time reading. Lev writes articles in Russian about art, music—almost any subject. He is very creative.

Irene worries about her parents, particularly about her mother. Tatyana gets homesick so often. She misses the active life she led in Russia.

Irene keeps looking for a good English class that her parents can take near their home. Because neither Lev nor Tatyana drives, getting to and from classes would be difficult. But Irene hasn't given up hope. She wants her parents to be happy and knows that being able to speak English would make them happier here in America.

(Above left) *Michael, Lev, and Tatyana chat during dinner.* (Above) *Tatyana enjoys reading newspapers and other materials printed in the Russian language.*

The Shurovs still keep in touch with Bella, Irene's former employer. Boris, Irene, and Michael visit Bella at the nursing home where she lives.

 Both Irene and Michael struggled to find challenging work once they arrived in the United States. In Russia, Irene was an activities director at a music school for children between the ages of 7 and 15. She conducted the choir and taught piano. But her musical career almost ended in the United States. No one would hire her because she did not speak English.

Irene took a job helping a woman named Bella, who has a disease called multiple sclerosis (MS). Even though her father was a doctor, Irene knew almost nothing about MS, which cripples the central nervous system. "It was my job to put Bella in bed, put her in a wheelchair, put food on the table," Irene explains. "Bella had a lot of patience. She helped me with my English. And she let Boris join us on the weekends, when I stayed at Bella's apartment."

Bella became a dear friend. She made Irene's new life much happier. "I worked for Bella for two years," Irene says. "She was wonderful to both Boris and me."

Irene stopped working for Bella after getting a job as a manicurist. She could earn more money and spend more time with her family.

Bella is 77 years old. Her health is getting worse. "It is so sad," Irene says. "We don't see her very often . . . . We miss her."

In 1993, after more than three years in America, Irene got a job as a music therapist at a Jewish center in Chicago. Irene works with people who have Alzheimer's, an incurable disease that destroys a person's memory. "My music really helps," Irene says. "I play and sing American songs. Their mood changes. I love my job."

Michael's work as a visual artist in America is not as satisfying. Before becoming a refusenik, Michael was a top film and television director in Russia. In the United States, he makes do with any assignment he can get. Michael photographs and videotapes Jewish weddings and other celebrations. He works with film producers as an assistant director. And he plays jazz piano at social

A talented pianist, Irene found work as a musical therapist a few years after arriving in the United States.

Michael works as a cameraman at a Polish television station in Chicago.

events. His photography has appeared in both of Chicago's daily newspapers and has been shown in an exhibition.

"I do anything for a living," Michael says. "I'm not a major film director. And I worry a lot about making enough money for my family and me. But I still feel very lucky. I live in America. I can show my Jewish feelings in my work. I have my freedom."

Michael appreciated that freedom even more after a trip back to Russia in 1993. He went to look at film footage that had recently been declassified, or made public. Up until that time, the films had been kept secret.

Michael was amazed. He viewed footage of prison inmates on death row and of bloody military fighting. He watched an interview with cosmonaut Yuri A. Gagarin, the first man in space.

Michael was able to bring some of the best footage back to America. He planned to sell the film to U.S. producers of television and film projects.

Getting through Russian customs (the agency that examines luggage looking for unclaimed goods being taken in or out of a country) was not easy. "It was a nightmare," Michael recalls. "The Russian government did not know I had the footage. If the people at customs had opened my luggage and found the film, I could have been in big trouble. Exactly what kind of trouble, I'm not sure.

A film and television director by trade, Michael also plays jazz piano at social functions as well as for his own pleasure.

"As it was, it took 25 minutes before I made it through customs. A customs agent said I didn't have the right papers to allow me out of Russia. But I looked the agent straight in the eyes. I didn't want him to think I was scared. I didn't want him to suspect anything. It worked. Finally, they said I could board the plane back to America. I was very lucky."

 In the Soviet Union, the Shurovs were not allowed to practice their religious traditions. Since coming to the United States, Boris and his family celebrate Jewish holidays such as Hanukkah, the Festival of Lights. The holiday begins on the 25th day of the Hebrew month of Kislev. This day falls either at the end of November or sometime during December.

39

The story of Hanukkah begins more than 2,000 years ago in Judaea, a region that included part of what is now Israel. Judaea was occupied mostly by Jews. At that time, King Antiochus IV (also called Epiphanes) of Syria ruled Judaea. He demanded that the Jewish people worship Greek gods as he did. He turned the Temple of Jerusalem, a place sacred to the Jews, into a Greek place of worship.

But the Jews had prayed to a single god, Jehovah, for centuries and refused to pray to the Greek gods. Antiochus decided to punish the disobedient Jews. He said they would be put to death unless they gave up their religion.

One day a rabbi named Mattathias encouraged the Jews to fight Antiochus's troops. Mattathias and other villagers left their homes to fight the Syrians. When Mattathias grew too old for battle, his son Judah took his place. Mattathias, Judah, and his brothers were called the Maccabees, which, in Hebrew, the language of the Jews, means "hammer."

The day the Maccabees recaptured Jerusalem from the Syrians, Judah and his army destroyed the statues of the Greek gods in the temple. Then the men made the temple a house of prayer to their own god again. To celebrate, the Maccabees declared a holiday called Hanukkah, which means "dedication" in Hebrew.

Years later, a legend became

The Shurovs gather in their Chicago home for a Hanukkah celebration. Hanukkah, a Jewish holiday that was not formally recognized by the Soviet government, is relatively new to the Shurovs, who didn't practice the tradition in Russia.

part of the Hanukkah story. No one knows how it began. The legend says that for the first Hanukkah celebration, the rabbis wanted to light their holy lamps. In Biblical times, lamps were filled with olive oil, and a wick soaking in the oil was burned to light the lamps. In the Temple of Jerusalem, however, the rabbis found one small jar with just enough oil to burn for one night.

They poured the jar of oil into the lamp. But instead of burning for only one day, the oil kept on burning . . . two days, three days, four days. The oil lasted for eight days—long enough for the rabbis to get a new supply. And that is why Hanukkah lasts for eight days.

(Left) *Boris and Irene prepare latkes for a Hanukkah dinner.* (Bottom) *After eating, the Shurovs will open gifts.*

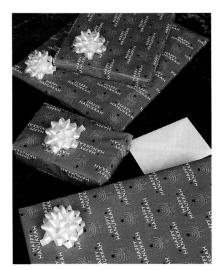

In the United States, the Shurovs, like many Jews, celebrate eight days of Hanukkah. Each night they light one candle in a Hanukkah menorah (a nine-branched candleholder). Then they eat special holiday foods. One favorite Hanukkah dish is called latkes, or potato pancakes. Boris sometimes helps his mother make the delicious dish for the whole family to enjoy.

Hanukkah is also a time for giving and receiving gifts. Friends gave Boris a book about Michael Jordan. They know how much he loves and admires the sports figure, whom Boris would call the greatest basketball player ever. Boris was thrilled with the book. He had a hard time putting it down.

Nick received a new winter shirt. The shirt had a high collar and buttons down the front. It reminded the Shurovs of shirts that Russians used to wear in the 1800s.

Everyone enjoyed being together to celebrate Hanukkah. They talked, laughed, and gave thanks for their freedom. Tatyana seemed very happy. The celebration made her forget her sadness. She had a twinkle in her eye and love in her heart.

Nick holds up his present—a shirt that resembles the fashion in nineteenth-century Russia.

A good cook, Irene often makes a traditional Russian soup called borscht.

44

Boris pets Chloe, the family cat.

 Irene still cooks Russian meals for her family. "Most Russians eat soup at least once a day," Irene explains. "So we eat a lot of soup." Vegetable soup, pea soup, and either a beet or a cabbage soup called borscht are some of the family's favorites.

"And we eat a lot of potatoes," Boris says. "And blintzes. We can't forget blintzes." Blintzes are thin, rolled pancakes filled with cheese, vegetables, or meat.

The Shurovs prepare all kinds of meat. And cabbage is a staple. Irene sometimes boils the cabbage. Sometimes she fries it.

While the Shurovs often enjoy Russian meals at home, America's fast food is what interests Boris. "I love McDonald's," Boris says. "And I like pizza. There is no pizza in Russia."

 Soon after the 1994 Hanukkah celebration, Boris's grandfather Lev suffered a stroke. Lev was rushed to the hospital in an ambulance. Part of his brain tissue had been destroyed. Lev lost his sense of balance, and he could not walk.

Lev recovered at a hospital far from the Shurov's home. Because of the long commute, the family did not visit him as often as they wanted to. And because he could not speak English, Lev could not tell the doctors and nurses exactly how he was feeling.

The doctors thought that Lev might be able to walk again. But he did not agree. After all, he was a doctor who had worked with stroke patients in Russia.

Lev was right. Even though he was allowed to leave the hospital and move to a nursing home, he could not walk. And then, early in 1995, Lev had another stroke that left him paralyzed and unable to talk.

During this time, Irene cried about her father every day. "It is terrible . . . just terrible," she would say. "I don't know what to do. We go to visit him as often as we can. But I don't think he's going to get better. It is heartbreaking."

After Lev's first stroke, Tatyana began staying with Boris and his family. "Why did I come to America if I could not live with you?" she asked Irene in Russian.

Tatyana is very close to her only daughter, Irene.

Boris sees a bright future in America. He is a "regular kid" who enjoys sports, math, science, and art. He takes swimming lessons three times a week. "I can swim," Boris says. "I'm taking lessons to swim better." He is also good at basketball, football, and biking.

Boris and his family recently moved into a new townhouse in a suburb of Chicago called Buffalo Grove. The house is near a pond and a park. Boris and his friends spend a lot of time playing in the park, even in bad weather. "The weather in Leningrad was horrible!" Boris exclaims. "It was really, really cold. There was lots of snow. Believe it or not, winters in Chicago are a lot nicer."

(Above) *Boris and Nick are in the yard of the family's Buffalo Grove home.* (Right) *Boris executes a fine backstroke in the school pool.*

Boris waits at a neighborhood park to play basketball with his friends.

(Above) *Many of the subjects Boris studies in his U.S. classroom would have been part of his course work in Russia, too.* (Right) *Boris enjoys sports, including soccer, a popular game in Russia.*

During a geography lesson, Boris points to the ocean he crossed to reach the United States.

Several other Russian families live in Boris's neighborhood. "I don't know why," Boris says. "But it's good. I play with the Russian kids and with American kids. I have lots of friends."

The Shurovs moved to Buffalo Grove because the schools there are good. "Education is important," Irene reasons. "We want Boris to have the best. The schools in Chicago have some big problems. We didn't want to worry about Boris. Here, the schools are safe. The

Like his father and mother, Boris is artistic. He spends a good deal of time drawing in his sketchbook.

classes are smaller. Children can learn as much as they want."

Boris has met the challenge of living in a different culture. He is an excellent student who gets very good grades. And he works hard. "I spend two to four hours on homework every night," he notes. One thing Boris does not get enough of at his new school is art. "I love to draw," he says. He opened his sketchbook with great pride. There were drawings of basketball players dunking the ball. There was a beautiful sketch of a young girl.

Does Boris dream of being a great artist someday? "No," he says. "I want to be a pro basketball player. I play the game as often as I can, sometimes several hours a day. My father is tall. That should help." And if he doesn't make the pros? "If I don't make it, I'd like to be a doctor."

Boris knows that if he were still living in Russia, he would not have had the freedom to realize his dreams. "I never would have known the game of basketball like I know it here," he says. "And, in Russia, you can't always choose what you want to be."

Boris doesn't skip a beat when asked if he would like to live in Russia again. "Someday, if it gets better in Russia, I would like to visit," Boris says. "But I am an American now. This is my home. This is where I will stay."

(Bottom) *Boris boards the school bus for home, where he will follow his routine of study, sports, and family time.* (Left) *Basketball became Boris's passion in life shortly after he came to the United States.*

53

PRONUNCIATION GUIDE

Alzheimer's (AHLTS-hy-muhrz)
Antiochus (an-TY-uh-kuhs)
borscht (BAWRSHT)
czar (ZAHR)
Dostoyevsky, Fyodor (dahs-tuh-YEHF-skee, FYAWD-uhr)
Epiphanes (ih-PIHF-uh-neez)
Gorbachev, Mikhail (gawr-buh-CHAWF, mih-KYL)
Hanukkah (HAH-nuh-kuh)
Judaea (joo-DEE-uh)
latke (LAHT-kuh)
Leningrad (LEHN-uhn-grad)
Maccabees (MAK-uh-beez)
Mattathias (mat-uh-THY-uhs)
menorah (muh-NOHR-uh)
refusenik (rih-FYOOZ-nihk)
sclerosis (skluh-ROH-suhs)
Semitic (suh-MIH-tihk)
Shurov (SHUR-awv)
Tatyana (taht-YAH-nah)
Tchaikovsky, Pyotr Ilich (chy-KAWF-skee, PYAW-tuhr
   ihl-YEECH)

FURTHER READING

Burns, Marilyn. *The Hanukkah Book.* New York: Macmillan, 1984.

Carrion, Esther. *The Empire of the Czars.* Danbury: Children's Press, 1994.

Clark, Philip. *Russian Revolution.* North Bellmore, NY: Marshall Cavendish, 1988.

Gray, Bettyanne. *Manya's Story: Faith and Survival in Revolutionary Russia.* Minneapolis: Runestone Press, 1995.

Haskins, Jim. *Count Your Way through Russia.* Minneapolis: Carolrhoda Books, 1987.

Magasci, Paul R. *The Russian Americans.* New York: Chelsea House, 1989.

Moga, Jerome. *Mikhail Gorbachev.* New York: Bantam, 1991.

Russia. Minneapolis: Lerner Publications, Geography Department, 1992.

ABOUT THE AUTHOR

Jane Mersky Leder is an award-winning author and journalist whose books include *Brothers & Sisters: How They Shape Our Lives* and *Dead Serious: A Book for Teenagers about Teenage Suicide*. Ms. Leder has written magazine articles for numerous publications, including *Psychology Today, Good Housekeeping, McCall's, Glamour,* and *Woman's Day.* She has led workshops on teenage suicide and been recognized by the American Association of Suicidology. A native of Detroit, Ms. Leder resides in Evanston, Illinois, with her husband, Alan.

PHOTO ACKNOWLEDGMENTS

Cover photos by Eugene G. Schulz (left) and Alan Leder (right). All inside photos by Alan Leder except the following: Jeff Greenberg, pp. 6, 9, 12; © Vladimir Pcholkin/FPG International, p. 7; Minneapolis Public Library and Information Center, p. 8 (both); Laura Westlund, pp. 16, 26; Patrick Hammill, p. 17; National Archives, photo no. 165-WW-157D-3, p. 18 (top); Independent Picture Service, p. 18 (bottom); © Wolfgang Kaehler, p. 19; National Archives, photo no. 306-NT-171445C, p. 20 (left); UPI/Bettmann, p. 20 (right); American Petroleum Institute, p. 21; Russell Adams, p. 22; © SYGMA, p. 23; Karen Sirvaitis, p. 25; Grant H. Kessler, p. 27 (left); Cut-ins: Details from a series of stained-glass windows by Marc Chagall, courtesy of Minneapolis Public Library and Information Center